WOVEN WORKS

BY JOHN AND SUSAN HAMAMURA

Chronicle Books/San Francisco
A Prism Edition

For Billie and Arthur.

Library of Congress Cataloging in Publication Data

Hamamura, John.
    Woven works.

    "A Prism edition."
    Bibliography: p.
    1. Fiberwork. 2. Weaving. I. Hamamura,
Susan, joint author. II. Title.
N7433.9.H35   746.1'4   78-17163
ISBN 0-87701-118-4

Book and cover design by Catherine Flanders.
Chronicle Books
870 Market Street
San Francisco, CA 94102
A Prism Edition

For information concerning the pieces in
this book or the individual artists
please contact John and Susan Hamamura
through their publishers.

"I dyed my yarns
  the same color as the sky at twilight
  that one magical summer day
  when I was nine years old . . ."
                              —Anonymous

This book is about contemporary fiber art; it is also about the relationship of some modern woven works to designs and techniques of the past. Though the pieces in this book have been arranged in technical, cultural, geographical or chronological groups, the placements are not meant to pigeonhole an artist or piece. The factors influencing any artist's creativity are far too complex to be so simply defined.

The concerns of contemporary fiber artists are so diverse they seem to defy definition. Some fiber artists work with metal, plastic, color Xerox, photo-screen emulsions, exploring how the newest technologies can alter the old forms and patterns. Other fiber artists delve backward in time, studying each intersection of warp and weft in some fragment of fabric unearthed in a Peruvian ruin, studying until they can translate that nameless weaver's message into contemporary terms.

Some fiber artists work on a monumental scale; others choose to form their pieces in miniature. Some hold to their art and craft with a fierce seriousness; others weave lightly, in humor and playfulness. Some produce three-dimensional sculpture; others create the illusion of depth on a flat plane.

Like a tree the ancient art and craft of weaving grows and differentiates into numerous branches. Yet all the diverse branches rise from the same root stock—rich with the maturity of many millennia of patient hands, vibrant still with yet unperceived potentials.

It was with the hope that we could further inspire and nurture the growth and diversity of this tree, that we produced this book.

John and Susan Hamamura

Susan Hamamura. Jus' Weavin' the Blues.
24 by 22 inches.
Wool and cotton card-woven bands
supplemented by brushed denim bands serve
as the weft in this double-woven piece.
It is turned sideways for hanging.

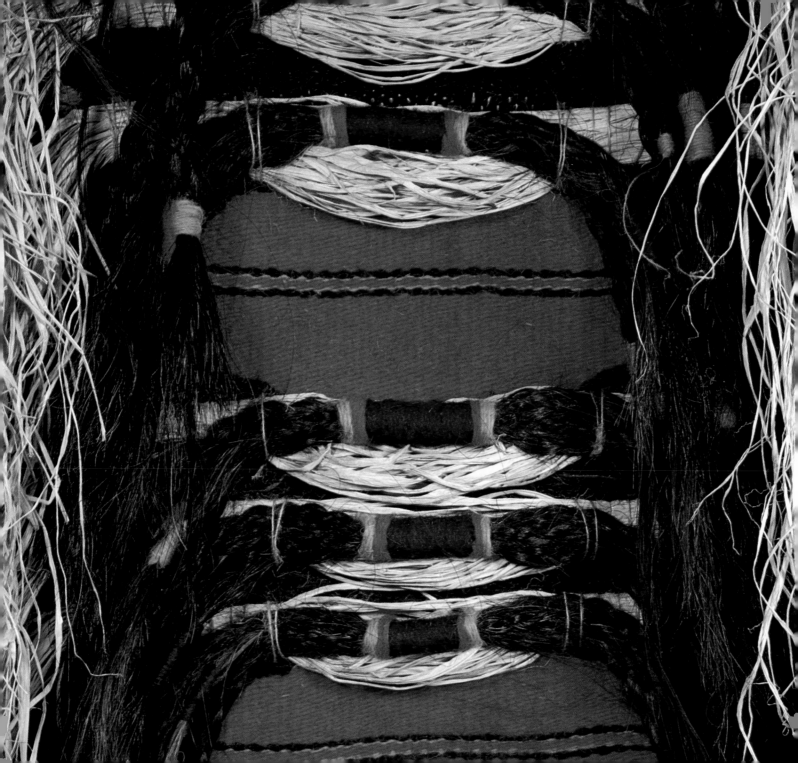

African weaving has served as the inspiration for some contemporary fiber artists. This African loom, from the collection of Inger Jensen, is from the Bamenda area of equatorial Cameroon. It was made and used predominantly by the men of the Bamileke Tribe. Their raffia weavings are usually made into mats or hunting bags.

Bonnie Britton. Africa. 9 by 5 feet.
A wool, raffia, horse hair, and jute tapestry
with braiding, from the collection of
Jeanne L. Epping.

Weaver Unknown. 29 by 9 inches.
A plain weave raffia mat of the Ibibio Tribe
in Nigeria from the collection of the Lowie
Museum of Anthropology, University
of California, Berkeley.

Bonnie Britton. Sky Log. 32 by 18 inches.
Dyed and felted wool. Felt is made when
the woolen fleece is alternately shocked by
drenching it with hot and cold water.
This process, combined with pressure,
causes the fibers to interlock and bond
together into a tight mass.

Bonnie Britton. Untitled. 42 by 18 inches.
Dyed, felted wool and rayon needle
weaving.

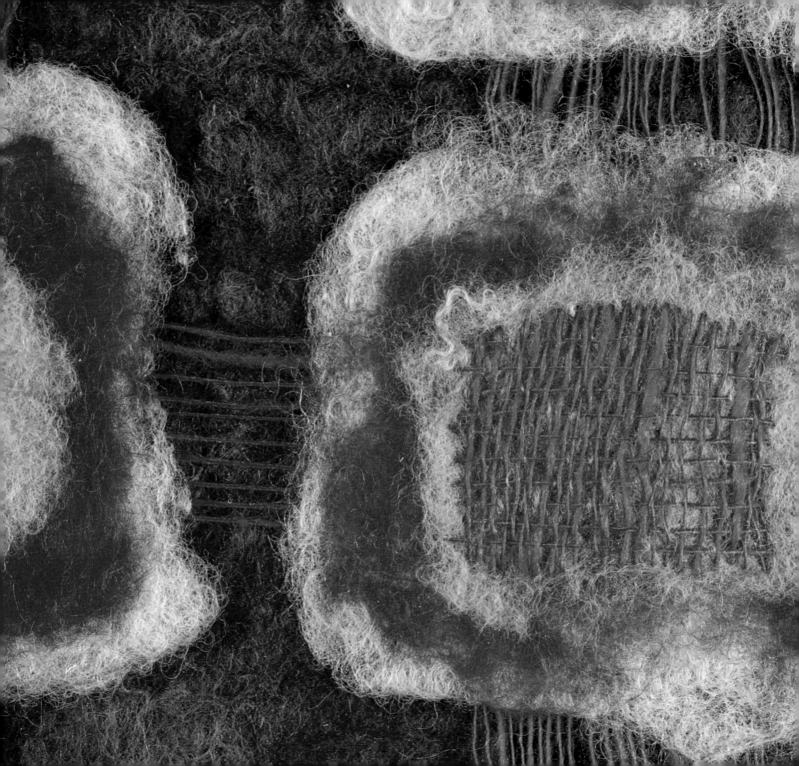

Middle Eastern tradition has supplied modern fiber artists with a number of techniques, including split-ply twining and soumak, that can be seen in some of the following pieces. Card weaving is also an ancient method in which flat cards are used instead of a loom. These cards—some of the oldest of which have been unearthed in China—are usually square and have a hole punched in each corner through which the yarns are threaded.

Bettie Adams. Persian Dream.
56 by 24 inches.
An assemblage of separate card-woven bands, in which some of the bands were sewn, others woven together so that the warp or lengthwise threads of one band become the weft or cross threads for another.

Ann Dizikes. Untitled. 29 by 29 inches.
Card-woven bands close the two sides
of the twined body of the cushion above.
The warp of the twining becomes the weft
of the card-woven bands.

Lillian Elliott. Song of Songs. 36 by 48
inches, opposite.
A wool and linen tapestry in Hebraic
calligraphy. The passage, from the "Song of
Solomon," reads: ". . . for lo, the winter
is past, and the rain is over and gone.
The flowers appear on the earth, the time of
singing has come and the voice of the
turtledove is heard in our land."

Candace Crockett. River God. 7 by 10 feet.
Bands were individually card woven using
overspun wool, mohair and camel hair
yarns and were then sewn together by hand
to create the piece.

Lynne Giles. Untitled. 30 by 20 inches. Double-faced card-woven bands of wool and camel hair, sewn together.

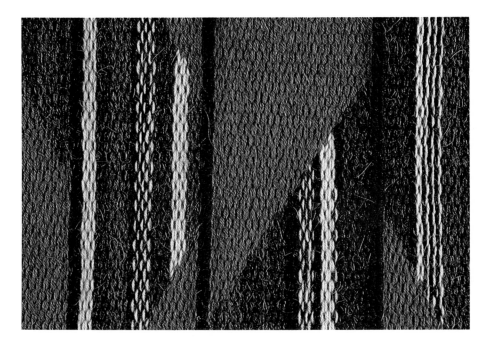

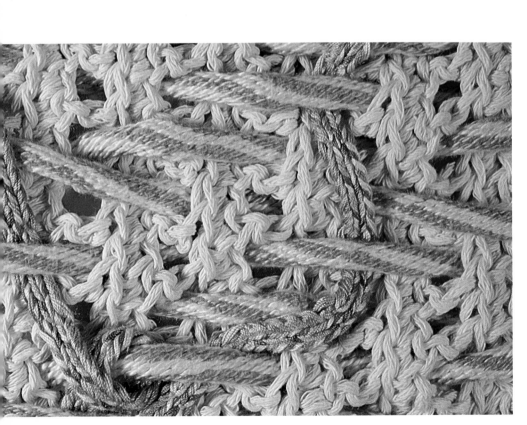

Susan Hamamura. Friends. 11 by 7½ inches. Cotton and silk card-woven bands interwoven through a network of crocheted cotton. From the collection of the Richmond Art Center.

Susan Hamamura. Wind. 11 by 7 inches. Cotton, linen, silk, and raffia loom-woven with embroidered French knots. From the collection of Dr. and Mrs. Charles A. Nelson.

Susan Hamamura. Twill.
27½ by 11½ inches.
This piece, shown in detail, is of
wool and cotton card-woven bands
interwoven in a 2/2 twill—the weft passed
over two warp bands, then under two.

Inger Jensen. Waves. 56 by 37 inches. A wool and rayon gauze and double weave in which the modulation and interaction of the two layers of fabric are particularly evident.

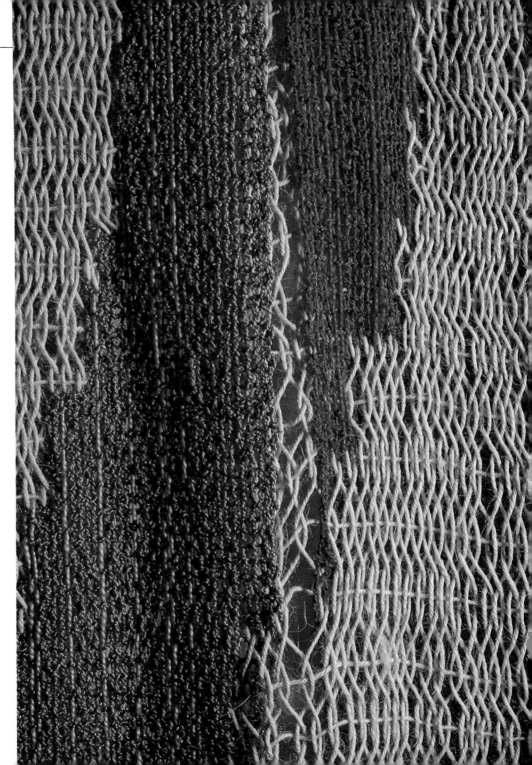

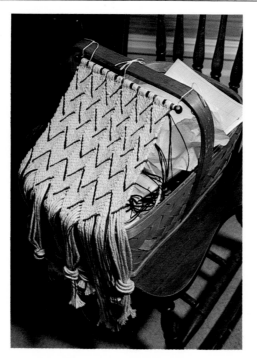

Kay Sekimachi. Variations on a Camel's Girth #3. 21 by 7 inches, detail, left. The split-ply twining technique for these pieces was taken from camel girth bands of Northern India. To make this series the artist attached each warp to a dowel hung from a basket handle, placed the basket on her lap and twined the piece.

Kay Sekimachi. Variations on a Camel's Girth #7. 20 by 7 inches, right. Cotton, split-ply twining.

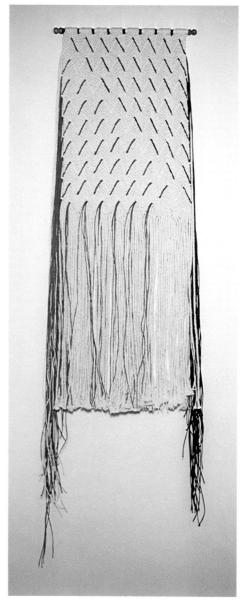

Kay Sekimachi. Linen Tapestry Boxes.
Tapestry Boxes. 7½, 6½ and 5½ inches.
Ten-harness, double weave with pick-up,
using a continuous quadruple weft.

Anne H. Blinks. Untitled.
3 inches by 6 feet.
Two ends of a long one-weft,
double-weave band, in which the two
layers are woven simultaneously. The design
colors on one side become the background
colors on the other as shown. In this band,
the design on the left is of Turkish origin;
the one on the right is Bedouin.

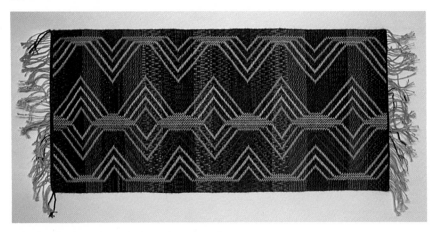

Martha Stanley. Untitled. 24 by 42 inches.
A tie-dyed and tapestry woven rug in wool
and linen done in the ancient Turkish
rug-weaving technique called soumak, in
which the warp threads are wrapped by the
threads of the weft.

Martha Stanley. Serpentine Rug.
24 by 36 inches.
Wool, camel, goat and mohair card woven
and combined with one-weft double
weaving technique.

Jane C. P. Veale. Untitled. 36 by 24 inches.
A double weave with pick up.

South American—particularly Peruvian—textile designs and techniques have been and continue to be a major source of inspiration for contemporary fiber artists. The influence of Peruvian motifs—as in the border curls used along the top of the detail on the facing page—is evident in this piece. The same type of border ornamentation can be seen in the Peruvian piece on the next page.

Maggie Sciarretta Potter. Spacemen.
30 by 30 inches.
A wool and mohair tapestry in which the reds were obtained from commercial dyes and the browns from walnut hulls.

Weaver Unknown. 19½ by 14 inches.
A cotton double cloth from the central
coast of Peru. From the Lowie Collection.

Weavers Unknown. 2½ inches wide,
above. 3 inches wide, right.
Details from Bolivian bands from the
collection of Joan Ward Summers.

Weaver Unknown.
A Bolivian chuspa or cocoa leaf bag,
from the collection of Joan Ward Summers.

Jacquetta Nisbet. Stele. 72 by 11 inches.
A wool Peruvian pebble weave. The fringe
was shaped by the clawing of the
artist's cat.

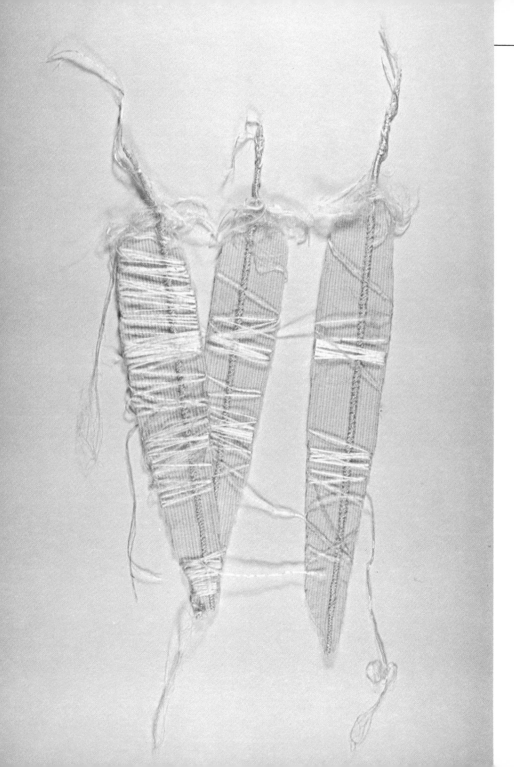

Jan Janeiro. Bound Feathers.
12 by 8 inches, left.
Linen and silk, shaped tapestry with
wrapping.

Jan Janeiro. In Memoriam: All the Small
Creatures. 12 by 8 inches.
A linen, silk and embroidery floss tapestry.

Weaver Unknown. 18 by 23 inches.
From the Nasca district in Peru—the Lowie
Collection.

Jan Janeiro. Peruvian Feather Pillow.
6 by 8 inches.
Linen, wool and feathers were used on the
tapestry and double-weave opposite.
Of her work the artist says: "My feather
pieces are a response to my studies of
Pre-Columbian Peruvian textiles . . . based
on the concepts of the fragmentary and
on a feeling for timeless simplicity."

Weaver Unknown.
Detail of a Peruvian poncho of wool and alpaca pebble weave, from the collection of Jacquetta Nisbet.

Weaver Unknown. 2 by 36 inches.
These parrots and the hummingbird in this Peruvian chain, top, from the Lowie Collection show the humor often seen in ancient pieces.

Jacquetta Nisbet. Untitled.
This Peruvian pebble weave and weft brocade band was woven on an inkle loom. The two-inch-wide band is linen, viscose and wool and was intended to be part of a shirt.

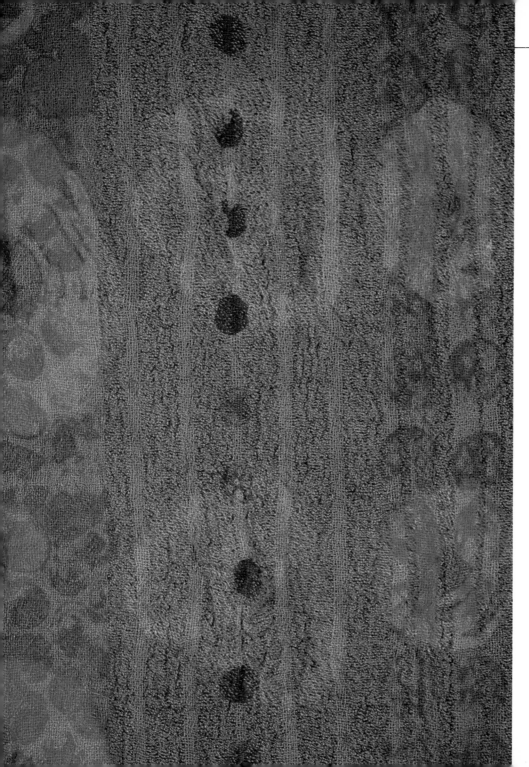

Lillian Elliott. Wedding Cloth.
36 by 30 inches.
This piece was first woven with highly
overspun cotton yarns with different
directions of spin. Tie-dying and block
printing were used to achieve
the final effect.

Nora Rogers. Growth. 36 by 22 inches. In addition to wool, this card-woven piece utilizes S-and-Z handspun camel and goat hair. By juxtaposing groups of counter-clockwise, or S-spun, warp yarns with groups of clockwise, or Z-spun, warp yarns, a special, subtle striping effect is achieved. The shape of the work was controlled by adding and then deleting warp threads, and by varying the tightness of the weft threads.

Scandinavian weaving techniques, including rya, have been widely adopted by modern fiber artists. Rya was traditionally used in the making of pile rugs; its basis is the Ghiordes knot, derived from ancient Turkish rug making. Designs and techniques are thus transmitted from weaver to weaver down through time, with each succeeding generation making a few alterations, reshaping the traditional elements to fit a personal vision of order and beauty.

Karen Tacang. Hair-itage Pillow.
24 by 15 by 6 inches, right.
Slentre, a Scandinavian braiding technique, was used in this card-woven pillow of wool, silk and human hair from four generations of the artist's Norwegian-American family.

Bonita Diemoz. Ruby Begonia.
19 by 20 inches.
The wool tapestry pillow cover opposite uses rya knots for Ruby's hair.

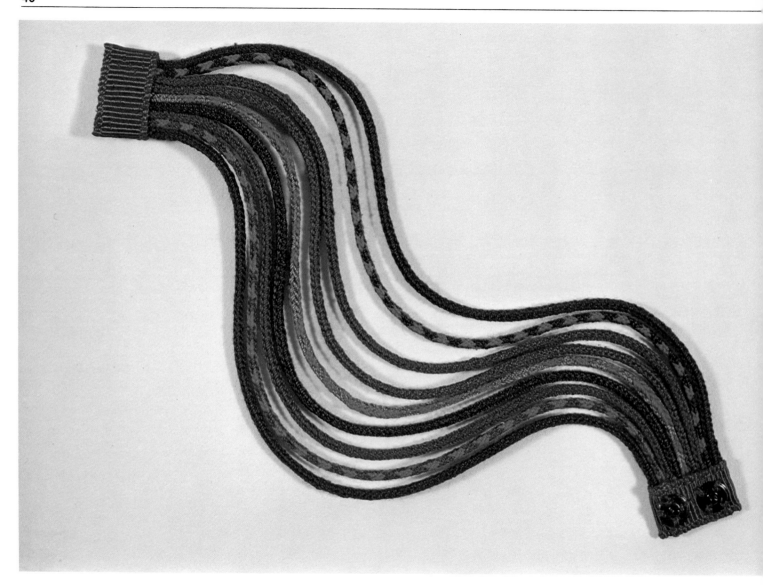

Susan Scott Bernal. Silk Slentre Bracelets.
8 inches in length.

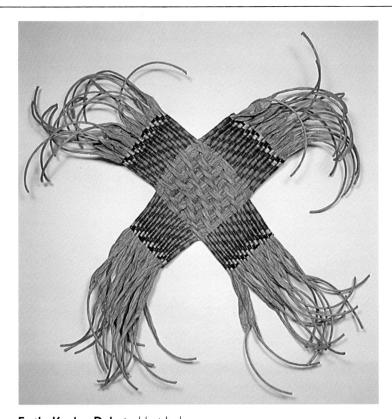

Emily Kardon Dubois. Untitled.
36 by 36 inches.
Ripsmatta, a Swedish warp-faced weave,
was used here with a plaited paper weft.
The paradox of this piece is that the plaited
center has been totally "woven-in"
by the wide cotton borders. Like a ship-in-
a-bottle or a carved ball in a wooden cage,
the outwardly simple design offers the
challenge of a wonderful puzzle.

Mary Pettis. Ralla. 18 by 5 inches.
The cotton "summer-winter" threading with
pickup used in this miniature weaving
was found in many early American coverlets.
The pattern areas in white appear as blue
on the reverse side of the fabric, so that the
coverlet could be changed with
the seasons.

Bonita Diemoz. Golden Fleece. 79 by
39 inches.
Wool and camel hair tapestry with fleece
rya knots.

Contemporary fiber artists take great pleasure in exploring new materials and new applications of old techniques. As in this piece, modern technologies have been put to work to alter the ancient forms and patterns. No medium—color Xerox, photo-screen emulsion, plastic, metal— is too new to be put to use.

Neda Al-Hilali. Untitled. 32 by 41 inches. Double-layer plaited industrial paper. Dyes and paints were applied before and after plaiting. The piece was then flattened by being run through a high-powered roller press.

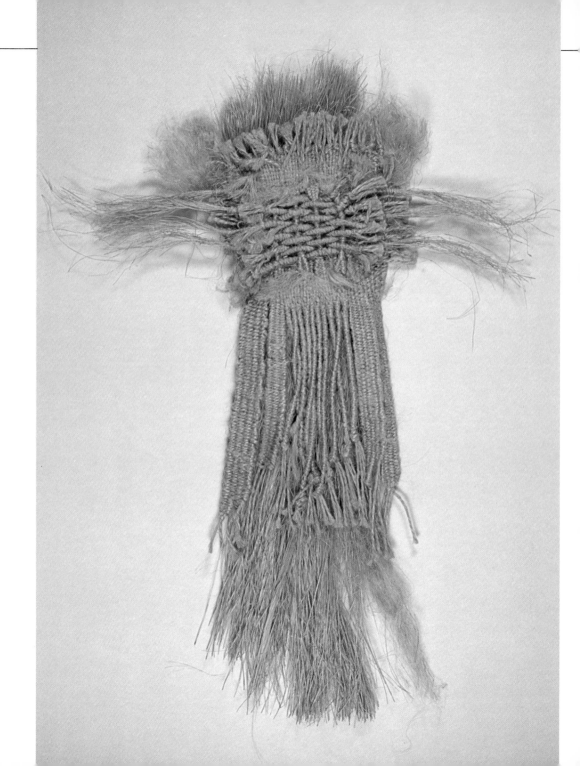

Marilou Mayo. Variation #4.
12 by 9 inches, left.
In this assemblage the artist has utilized linen
from all the stages of its processing—
from raw flax to its final spun form.

Marilou Mayo. Variation #5.
11 by 6 inches.
An assemblage of yak hair, beads, thread,
wool fleece and cotton string. One of the
artist's friends began making miniature
weavings and mailing them to friends as
"woven letters." Those letters partly
inspired the two miniature works shown
here.

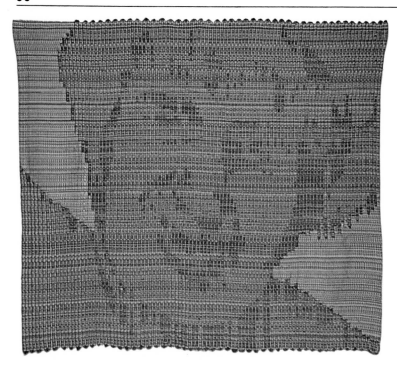

Victoria Barber. Dreaming. 33 by 29 inches.
The design for this commercially dyed
cotton weaving was drawn from a tiny
portion of a snapshot. The artist calls her
technique a warp-faced weave with the
warp threads almost entirely covering the
weft, and the warp colors determining the
design. When this piece is viewed from a
distance, it has a lavender cast to it,
yet as the detail reveals, this is an optical
illusion created by the juxtapositioning of
the complementary colors, blue and orange.
There are actually no purple or lavender
yarns used in the entire piece.

Linda Griggs. Indigo Sky I. 60 by 80 inches.
Linda Griggs. Indigo Sky II. 60 by 60 inches,
on the facing page.
Two wool, double-woven, stuffed
tapestries.

Marilou Mayo. Multiedges.
24 by 24 inches.
Woven wool strips, sewn together.

Maggie Sciarretta Potter. Split Warps.
11 by 11 inches.
A silk and handspun dog-hair tapestry.
The traditional definition of "tapestry," is a
handwoven fabric in which the weft
yarns cover the warp yarns completely, so
that the weft colors alone form
the design.

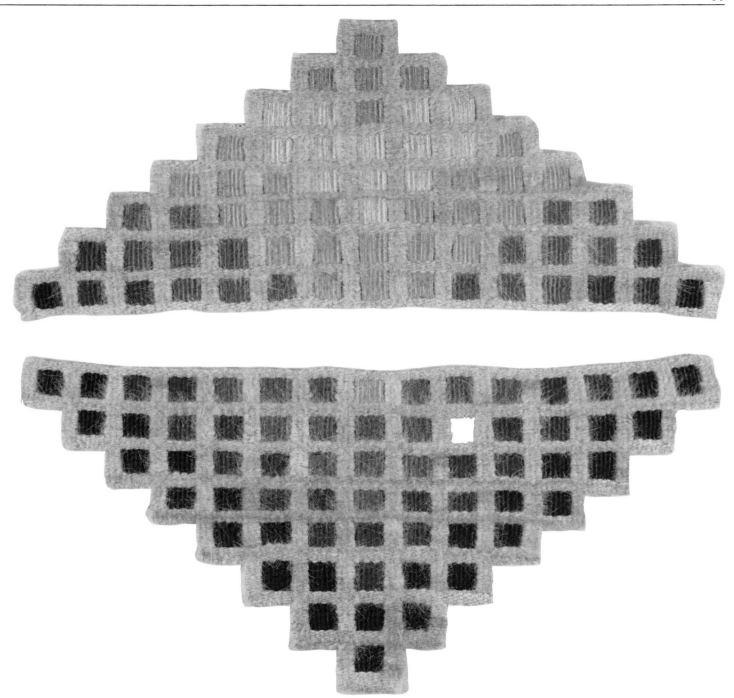

Neda Al-Hilali. Double Twist #105.
44 by 78 inches, left.

Neda Al-Hilali. Stacked Cubes.
38 by 72 inches.
Two tapestries of woven sisal.

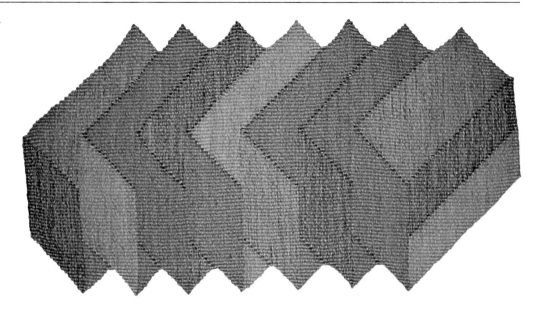

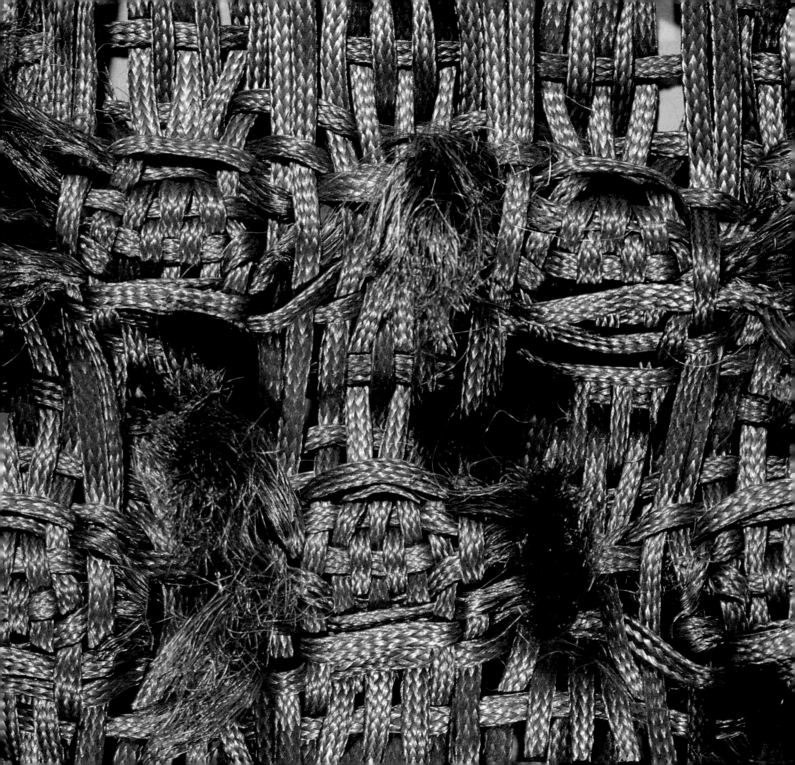

Karon Rucker. Untitled. 21 by 21 inches.
Waffle weave in detail. In this piece,
constructed of multi-stranded tinned copper
braid, the pattern sections were indepen-
dently warp weighted to allow them
to be drawn up during the weaving.

Gyöngy Laky. Untitled Study.
48 by 48 inches.
Tubular double cloth was first stuffed with
cotton batting, then plaited to form this
fiber sculpture.

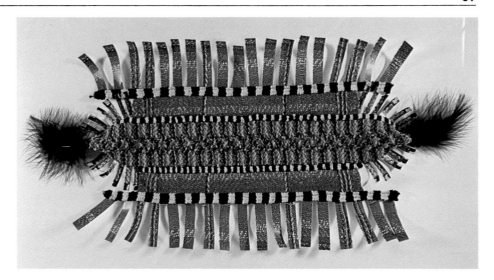

P. Charley. Feather Band. 12 by 24 inches.
An assemblage of rayon, feathers, cotton
and color-Xeroxed paper. The artist made a
full color-Xerox copy of part of the piece,
cut the Xerox into strips, then integrated
the strips into the final woven and
plaited work.

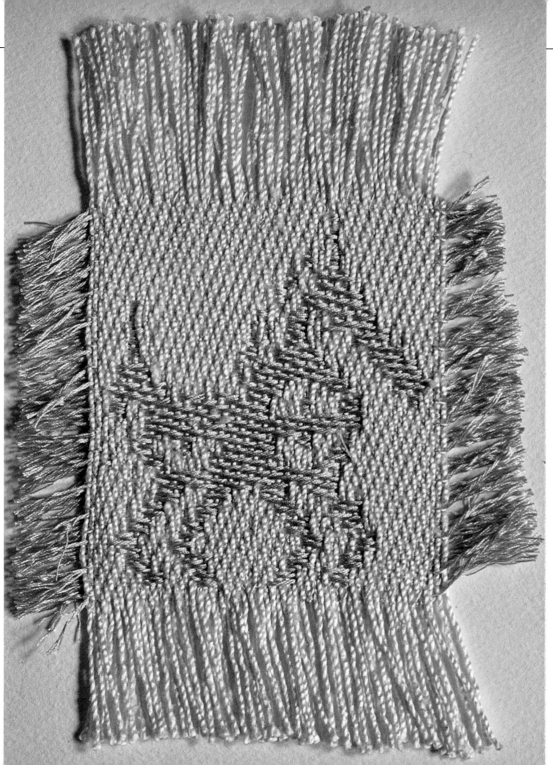

Lisa Mei Lee. Silk Horses.
One of a series of horse figures; the largest
is 9 by 9 inches and the smallest 3½ by
4 inches. Of them the artist says: "These
little horses were woven on a 40-harness
draw loom (32 pattern harnesses and 8 satin
weave harnesses). I usually pick my
figures—which lends fluidity. But for these,
I let the draw harness do all the work—
thus the 'stair-stepping' the rigidity—
but they're still quite playful, I think."

Lisa Mei Lee. Basket 2. 72 by 35 inches.
This silk brocade-on-linen design is an
optical illusion showing a basket from the
bottom and top simultaneously.

Judith Kohl. Untitled. 7 by 7 inches, left.
Perle cotton warp, baseball mitt weft.
Untitled. 7 by 11 inches, top.
Linen warp with copper wire, military
shirt and insignia weft. Twill weave.
Untitled. 7 by 7 inches.
Perle cotton warp with plastic gloves and
muslin rag weft. Pile weave.
"I began with the idea of weaving the type
of clothing that might be worn by and
echo the nature of a group of tyrants. The
idea took over, and the pieces seemingly
wove themselves and took their own forms.
They were done as a series on two separate
warps, all woven flat, then sewn into
their present forms. Although it was not a
consideration when I began, they needed
no special reinforcement to be free standing.
After they were finished, I saw them as
not very threatening, a little sweet
perhaps. . . ."

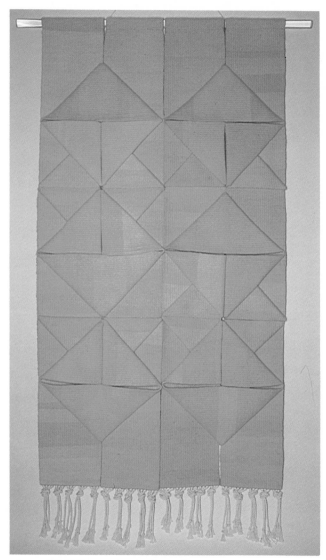

Anna Wolf. Simatu. 70 by 35 inches.
Hand-dyed wool was first woven into
strips, then folded and sewn together, and
cotton fringe added.

Karon Rucker. Cambia. 38 by 27 inches.
Dyed sisal. Crossing wefts in this double
weave allowed the artist to fan-fold the
piece after removing it from the loom.

Trude Guermonprez. We Are But Shadows.
40 by 36 inches.
In this cotton and wool double-weave
warp-print the two faces seen are photo-
screen printed images of the artist and her
husband. She used their images repeatedly
in a series of fiber works. Often the profiles
were tipped or turned in odd angles
that suggested mountain ranges, hearts or
other shapes.

Trude Guermonprez. Pale Heart.
45 by 52 inches, left.
A double weave warp-print of handspun
wool and cotton.

Trude Guermonprez. Quiet/Calm.
26 by 35 inches.
A double-weave warp-print of silk and
linen.

Trude Guermonprez. Leaves.
25 by 37 inches.
A silk, linen and handspun wool double-weave warp-print.
During her lifetime, 1910 through 1976, she won many awards including the prestigious American Institute of Architects Craftsmanship Medal for 1970. Her vision and commitment to excellence as a designer, weaver and educator have had enormous impact upon the direction of contemporary fiber art.

Weaver Unknown. 25 by 26 inches.
This detail of a painted fabric piece is from Trancas in the Nasca Valley of Peru. From the Lowie Collection.

Joan Ward Summers. New Mountain,
Old Mountain. 15 by 11 by 3½ inches.
This free-standing tapestry is framed in
stainless steel. One side (fully shown)
depicts ''New Mountain,'' the other side
(shown in the detail) is ''Old Mountain.''

Joan Ward Summers. Alaskan Midnight.
72 by 60 inches, right.
A wool and camel hair tapestry.

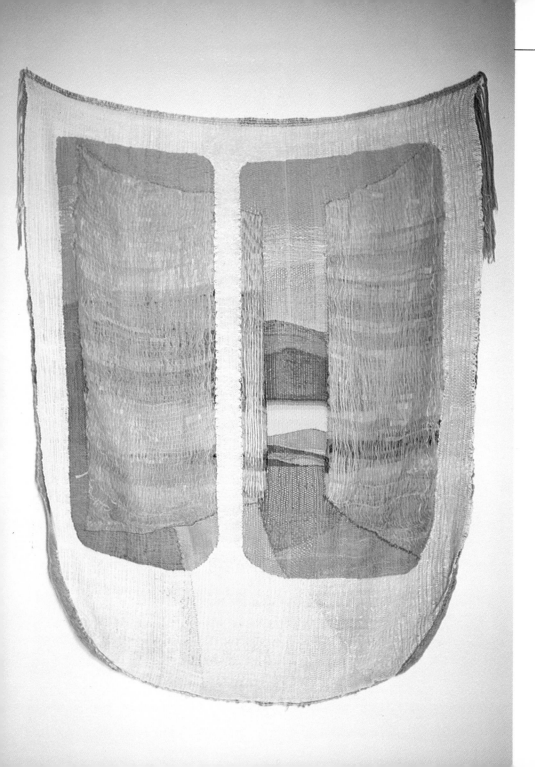

Janice L. Wagstaff. Window Landscape.
67 by 57 inches, left.
Multi-harness tapestry. These two works are
from a series of twenty "window/curtain"
pieces. According to the artist, the series
began "with a fascination for one of the
natural qualities of woven cloth—
that of draping. From there I became
interested in curtains, and then curtains in
relation to windows. I have used both real
windows to work from, as well as the
abstracted window form."

Janice L. Wagstaff. Light Well.
69 by 57 inches.
A cotton and rayon painted tapestry.

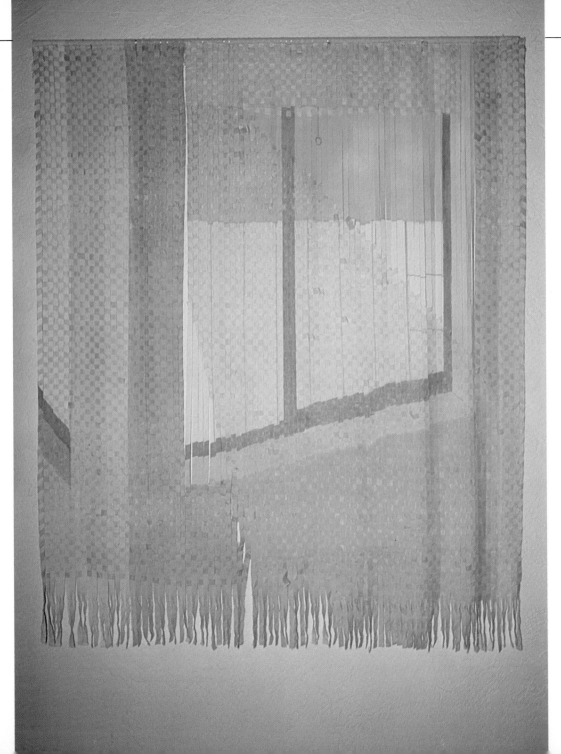

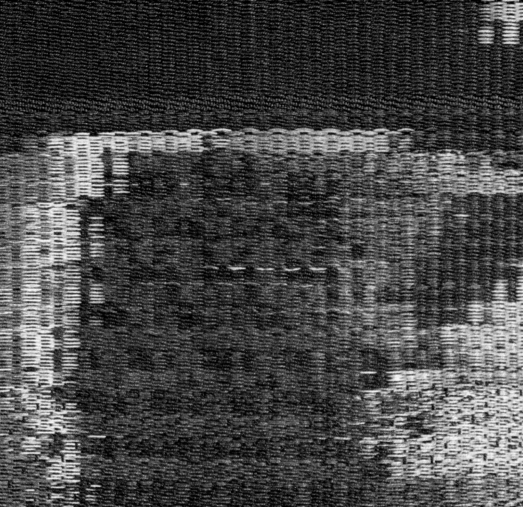

Japanese weavers have traditionally practiced the technique of ekasuri, also used in Southeast Asia, India, the Middle East and in Central and South America. In this country it is generally referred to as ikat—a process in which the warp and weft skeins are separately tied and dipped into the dye. The tied-off areas resist the color and when the threads are later woven up, the dye-resistant areas cross to form the design. "Perfect" image registration is impossible—hence the characteristic "wateriness" of the blocks, stripes or patterns.

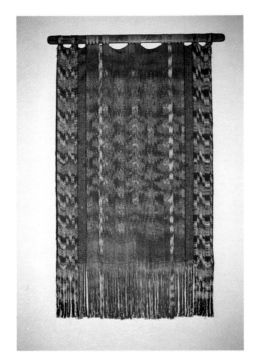

Jane Lackey. Untitled. Detail of a 36 by 50 inch panel from a triptych.

Jane Lackey. Untitled. 67 by 40 inches. Linen, rayon, silk and cotton ikat with overshot weave.

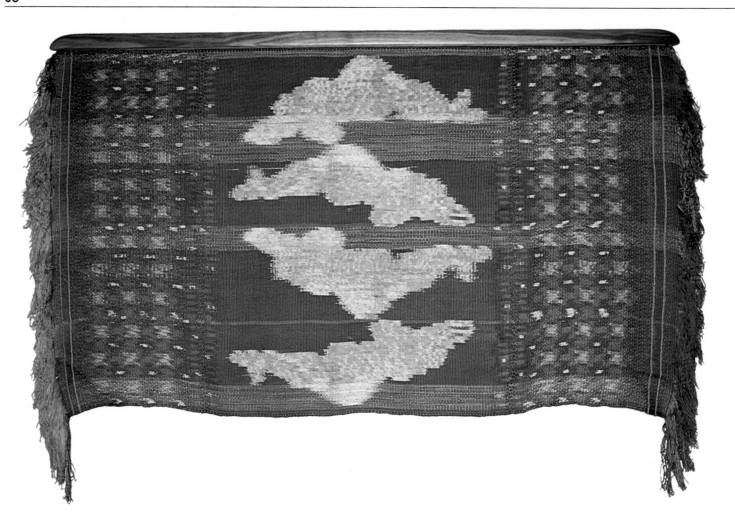

Jane Lackey. Suspension.
38 by 57 inches, left.
Linen, silk and rayon ikat with overshot
weave.

Tim Veness. Reflections of the Heart.
43 by 16 inches.
A partially stuffed cotton, four-harness,
double weave with pick up.

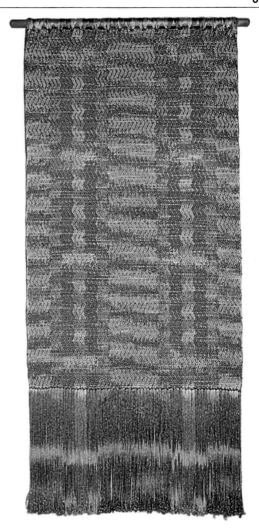

Tim Veness. Untitled. 51 by 23 inches.
The shimmering quality in this piece is due
to the use of rayon. The warp was ikat-dyed,
then woven as an eight-harness twill.

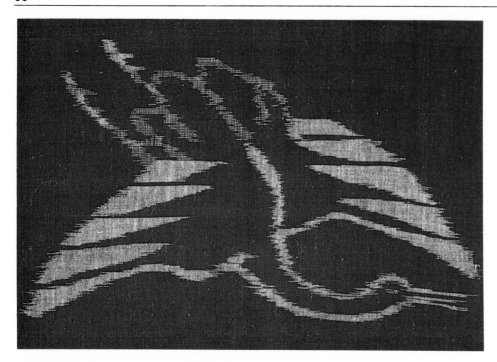

Weaver Unknown.
Indigo-dyed cotton ekasuri was used to
depict a crane on this futon from the
collection of Yoshiko Wada. The beautiful
blue of indigo dyed yarn is hard to achieve.
Indigo oxidizes extremely easily; vigorous
stirring or too much contact with the
open air can quickly exhaust a batch of dye.
Wet skeins of yarn have to be dipped with
care. To minimize oxidation excess dye
must be squeezed from the fibers while
they are still totally submerged. Successive
dippings—with time allowed between
for the yarn to dry—are necessary to achieve
the desired shade. The blue color develops
only when the yarn being dyed is
exposed to air; the color lightens as the
fibers dry.

Pat McGaw. Blue Fields. 35 by 29 inches.
Indigo-dyed ikat weft-faced panels joined
by cotton card-woven bands. The white
shapes were formed through the tight
binding of designated sections of the
undyed yarn—when the yarns were dipped,
the wrapped areas resisted the dye.

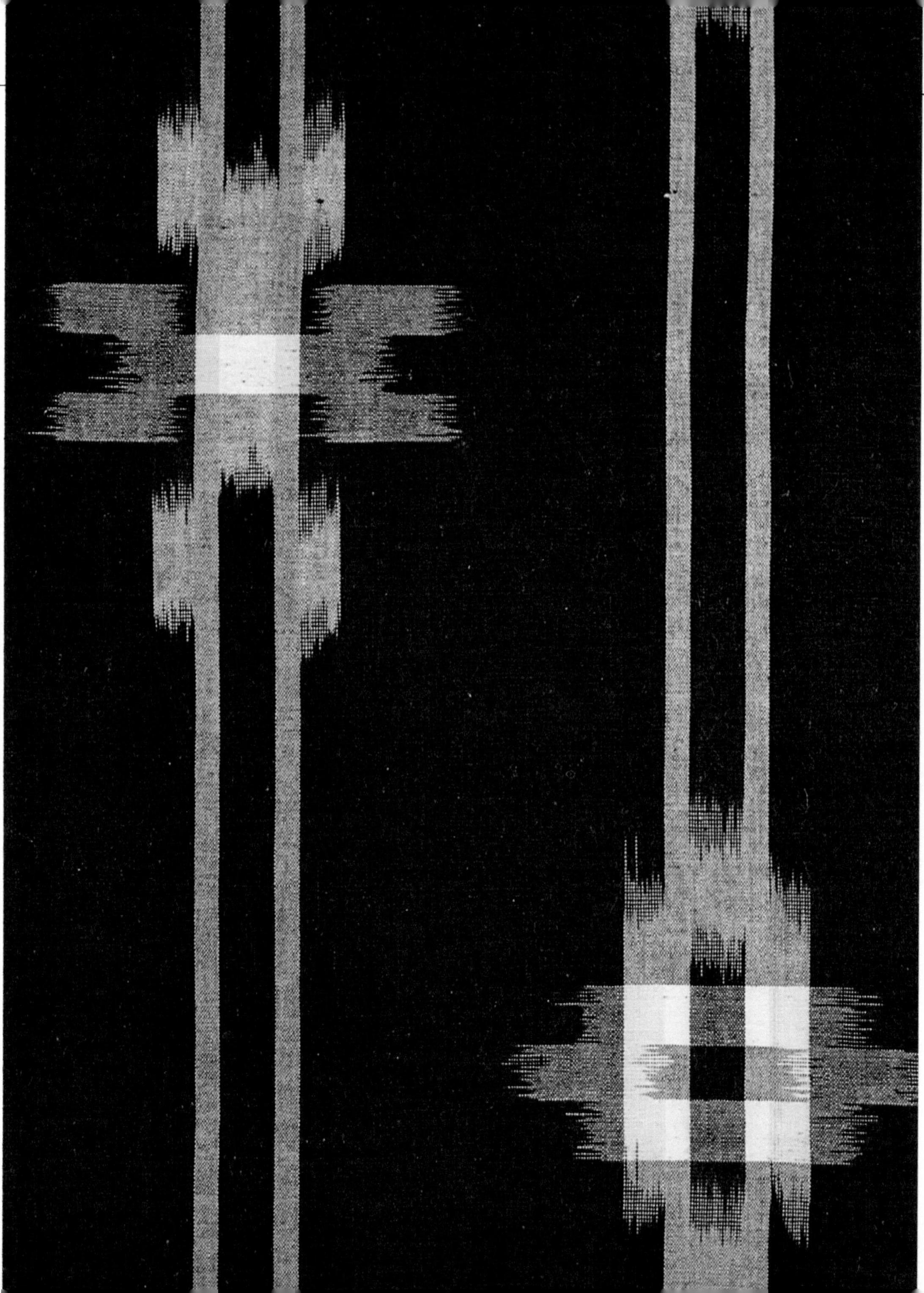

Weaver Unknown.
A detail from a Japanese futon of indigo-dyed cotton ekasuri, from the collection of Yoshiko Wada.

Weaver Unknown.
A carp, the Japanese symbol of perseverance, swims upstream in this indigo dyed cotton ekasuri. This piece is from the collection of Yoshiko Wada.

Proud weaver, shy weaver,
    how long can your heart persevere?
Silent weaver, laughing weaver,
    many blessings from your ancient sisters,
who knew, as you, life was the warp,
    their will the weft.
                        —Anonymous

The following materials were suggested by some of the artists whose works appear in this book. The materials are offered as avenues for deeper involvement in weaving and range from beginning to advanced categories.

Books

Albers, Anni.
ON WEAVING: Wesleyan University Press.

Andersen, Paulli.
BRIKVAEVNING: Borgens Forlag A-S. (Presently available only in Danish language edition)

Atwater, Mary M.
SHUTTLE-CRAFT BOOK OF AMERICAN HAND-WEAVING: Macmillan.

Black, Mary E.
NEW KEY TO WEAVING: Macmillan.

Cason, Marjorie and Cahlander, Adele.
THE ART OF BOLIVIAN HIGHLAND WEAVING: Watson-Guptill.

Collingwood, Peter.
THE TECHNIQUES OF RUG WEAVING: Watson-Guptill.

Crockett, Candace.
CARD WEAVING: Watson-Guptill.

D'Harcourt, Raoul. Denny, Grace G. and Osborne, Carolyn M.—Editors. Translated by Sadie Brown.
TEXTILES OF ANCIENT PERU AND THEIR TECHNIQUES: University of Washington Press.

Emery, Irene.
PRIMARY STRUCTURES OF FABRIC: Textile Museum.

Glashausser, Suellen and Westfall, Carol.
PLAITING STEP-BY-STEP: Watson-Guptill.

Harvey, Virginia.
SPLIT-PLY TWINING (Threads in Action Monograph Ser: No. 1) HTH Publications.

Larsen, Jack Lenor. Buhler, Alfred; Solyom, Bronwen and Garrett.
THE DYERS ART: Van Nostrand Reinhold.

Regensteiner, Else.
THE ART OF WEAVING: Van Nostrand Reinhold.

Ritch, Diane and Wada, Yoshiko.
IKAT: AN INTRODUCTION: Kasuri Dyeworks.

Trotzig, Liv and Axelsson, Astrid.
WEAVING BANDS: Van Nostrand Reinhold.

Turner, Alta R.
FINGERWEAVING: INDIAN BRAIDING: Sterling.

Periodicals

CRAFT HORIZONS
American Crafts Council
44 West 53rd Street
New York, NY 10019

FIBERARTS
3717 4th N.W.
Albuquerque, New Mexico 87107

HANDWEAVER AND CRAFTSMEN
220 Fifth Avenue
New York, NY 10001

SHUTTLE, SPINDLE AND DYEPOT
Handweavers Guild of America, Inc.
998 Farmington Avenue
West Hartford, CT 06107

We would like to thank the following for their time and cooperation:
  Allrich Gallery, San Francisco, California.
  Center for the Visual Arts, Oakland, California
  Discovery Gallery, Emeryville, California
  Los Robles Gallery, Palo Alto, California
  Source Gallery, San Francisco, California
We are especially grateful to the following people and institutions for their invaluable assistance during the preparation of this book:
  Pacific Basin Textile Arts, Berkeley, California
  Lowie Museum of Anthropology,
    The University of California, Berkeley
  Ann Dizikes
  John Elsesser
  Trudy Koeme
  Clinton MacKenzie
  Mary Martinez
  Frederick Mitchell
  Yoshiko Wada

WOVEN WORKS was printed on Warren's
Flokote by four-color process at
Cal-Central Press, Sacramento. Mackenzie-
Harris set the type in Kabel Light and Bold,
and Color Tech did the color separations.
The book design is by Catherine
Flanders. Editing is by Jane Vandenburgh
and production by R. C. Schuettge. The
binding was done by Cardoza-James,
San Francisco.